our *Life*
by FAITH

our *Life* by FAITH

Greg & Tonya Mills

TATE PUBLISHING
AND ENTERPRISES, LLC

Published by Tate Publishing & Enterprises, LLC
127 E. Trade Center Terrace | Mustang, Oklahoma 73064 USA
1.888.361.9473 | www.tatepublishing.com

Tate Publishing is committed to excellence in the publishing industry. The company reflects the philosophy established by the founders, based on Psalm 68:11,
"The Lord gave the word and great was the company of those who published it."

Book design copyright © 2013 by Tate Publishing, LLC. All rights reserved.
Cover design by Junriel Boquecosa
Interior design by Jomel Pepito

Published in the United States of America

ISBN: 978-1-62902-602-2
1. Biography & Autobiography / Personal Memoirs
2. Religion / Christian Life / Love & Marriage
13.10.16

Dedication

We dedicate this book to our Lord and Savior Jesus Christ and also to our children—Brandon, Ryan, Matthew, and Sarah—for all the joy you bring into our lives. We love you all very much and pray that your life follows God's plan.

Acknowledgments

Kelley McDade, thank you for everything you did; your input was invaluable.

Lori Lewis, thank you for listening to our story and placing the spark in our heart to share it with others.

Sam Simuzosha, thank you for all your prayers and encouragement.

Last but certainly not least, we want to thank our parents, family, friends, and colleagues who have been there for us throughout our lives encouraging, guiding, and just being there when we need you.

Contents

Introduction

Our life by faith began years before we ever met, and we had to grow in certain areas before the first meeting. God had his plan laid out, even with some mistakes and wrong roads; he knew we would one day meet, in his perfect timing, not ours. This is an incredible journey with the hand of God guiding the way, one step at a time. Now, let the journey into our life begin. Please be aware there are certain places we change narration within a chapter, this occurs to give a little more detail from the one who recalled it.

Gregory

My life began in a hospital in Beckley, West Virginia, on January 28, 1971; I was the firstborn son of Shirley and Karen Mills. My parents lived in a small house in Beckley at that time but eventually moved to a small apartment in Sophia, West Virginia, located approximately five miles south of Beckley. When I was between the ages of three or four, they moved to a house that they rented in Sophia for $100 a month. While living in Sophia, my parents became Christians, and this obviously would affect me and my life.

My childhood was typical. I attended school when it was in session. After school and summers were spent playing with my brother Matthew, who was seventeen months younger, and the neighborhood friends. I played baseball for the area little-league teams and loved it. In the winter, I would play basketball for the Sophia Christian Academy, the school from which I would eventually graduate from in 1989.

At the age of twelve, we were forced to move from our house in Sophia. My parents bought a house in the community of Coal City located about four miles away from Sophia. This home was a four-room house that was too small for our family. The first summer we lived at our new house, my dad remodeled it by tearing off the roof and adding a second floor. Between 1983 and 1984, a lot of things had changed in my life; the one thing that remained a constant, however, was our church attendance. My parents made us boys attend church with them. At times, I did not want to go. The older I got, the more I did not want to attend, especially on Wednesday and Sunday nights. Although I did not like it at the time, I am thankful my parents insisted that I attend church regularly. My parents' persistence paid off on October 25, 1988, my senior year of high school; I was saved and became a Christian. This was the best decision of my life.

Upon graduating high school, I enrolled at Beckley College. My plan was to get the basic courses at Beckley College for the first two years and then transfer to Concord College to receive my degree in education. I wanted to be a social studies teacher, just like my father. After enrolling at Concord, I loved attending the social studies and history courses but hated the education courses that were required to become a teacher. I chose to double major in history and geography, finishing my classes in 1993 but not graduating until 1995. (It is a long story, maybe in another book.)

My life during childhood through the school years were quite average to say the least. Some may even call my life up to this point dull and boring. I never partied or drank, even when my friends were doing such things. I dated a few girls from time to time but never married or had children. After finishing college, I got a job as an equipment salesman; not many people can say they had a job waiting for them after school, but I could. My cousin worked for a company and recommended me for the position of regional sales in southern West Virginia. It did not take long for me to realize that I am not a salesman. I am not outgoing or persuasive enough to be a good salesman. I held on to the job for a year, pretty much the calendar year of 1994, before I was let go. I am thankful for the opportunity at the sales job, but I learned never to try sales again as an occupation. In 1995, I had a couple of small, short-lived jobs with the local YMCA and for a magazine-distributing company. Early in 1996, I applied for a job at the local environmental testing laboratory. I remember going to the interview with a severe flu; I was so ill that my brother had to drive me. Despite the illness, the interview went well, and a week later, I received a call saying I had the job. This made me happy. I really wanted this job and could see myself working here for a long time to have some financial security and stability. On March 4, 1996, I began my new job at REIC Laboratory. This job opportunity was quite ironic because I disliked chemistry in school but now would be working on chemistry every day. God gave me this job for a reason;

however, it took more than eight years for the reason to become apparent.

These years were mostly good: I was young, in my twenties, moved away from home, played in various local sports leagues (basketball and softball). I also loved playing a game I first found at the age of fifteen, golf. I dated some ladies off and on during this period as well, but nothing serious. I had a lot of freedom and enough money to do things and go to places that I wanted. During these years, I had some tragedies and sadness—one being the death of a close cousin in 1994 and the other would be my parents' divorce in 1996. These two events had a profound effect on my life and my faith as well, making me a stronger Christian. During these years at the lab, I was reminded of the belief that I had gotten the job for a reason, and as the calendar turned to a new century, that reason would soon be revealed.

Tonya

April 22, 1975, was a great day—well, for me anyway. It was the day when I, Tonya Lee Earehart, was born to the proud parents of Charles Thomas Earehart and Patricia Lee Burgin Earehart. They did not quite know what they were getting into since their firstborn daughter, Christy, my elder and favorite sister, was not as vocal. I must also mention I have a baby sister, Ashley, ten years younger, who is my favorite youngest sister. Well, getting back to the story, I cried a lot, for most of my entire first year, which actually made my mom a basket case. Well, I do not remember this time in my life, so I'm not so sure my recollections are accurate, so let's go on to a time I do remember.

My earliest memories bring me to learning about God and how he loves me. Growing up in church shaped me and has had such an impact on the person I would become. I have had an interesting journey. This journey with the Lord began on May 2, 1983. When I was barely eight years old, I knew I wanted Jesus to be my Lord and Savior. I felt a comfort with him I cannot explain, just peace.

Over the next ten years or so, I guess I was a typical child with some advantages. We were not rich by any means, but our family had all we ever needed, and most of our wants were taken care of as well. Some thought we were rich, but my parents just managed money well, meeting our needs. At the age of fifteen, I began to work for my grandfather at the car dealership. I washed cars, filed paperwork, and did other odds and ends. As a typical teen, I ran around with my friends, hanging out at the mall on weekends and dated a few guys—some good ones and some bad ones. I cannot say that I have lived a perfect life free of sin, but I am a saved sinner. The mistakes I made in my teenage years have been forgiven and counted as lessons learned for the time being.

I went to college when I was nineteen to finish my degree in drafting and design. During this time, I began dating a guy who would become my first husband. He was somewhat older by nearly seventeen years. He had been married but was a widower at an early age, leaving him with two young children to raise. We met at the car dealership where we both worked. One thing led to another, and we became quite close. I also fell in love with his children. They hold a big place in my heart to this day, and they always will. We married after dating a year and a half, but we both knew deep down it would not last. We never asked God if this was his plan, and obviously it was not. We had some rough years, and I must say I ended it in an ungodly manner where I was at fault and have since asked God to forgive me. We were blessed with two wonderful boys in our seven years together, and I would not trade that time for anything. I feel we have grown to be better parents, and the boys see us getting along instead of fighting all the time.

There's a quotes that goes, "That which does not kill us makes us stronger." I know a few people who wanted to kill me a time or two during this period of my life, myself included. This next part is pretty hard to write but must be said, and you will see why later.

When I left my husband, I was unfaithful and knew I would never forgive myself nor would I ever be forgiven by him. I was talking to an old high school boyfriend, one of the bad guys of the past, although we never actually went on a date until after I was separated. We secretly talked on the phone and met at different places to talk. This was just as sinful as going on a date. The Lord knew all the mistakes I was about to make over the next few months; however, he was prepared to set his plan in motion to humble me. I knew this new relationship was set up to fail, but I was prepared to give it a good try. We started dating. We spent a lot of time together over the summer, but there was never much trust. I felt I had to watch him, because he did call a married woman. Since he had low morals, what would keep him from cheating on me with someone else? I was never at peace. I knew he was not right for me, but I dated him anyway. Soon I would be hit with a bomb. He was seeing someone else behind my back. Imagine that. He didn't really care. He was just a predator out to please himself. He did not care whom he hurt in the process. I found out it was someone I knew. She was a minor, not even old enough to legally date. How could he, and to beat it all, he lied to my face even when I caught him red-handed. I could have ruined his life. I seriously thought of ways to do it, but thankfully my wonderful family and friends talked me out of it.

Here is where I realized God was making my path. Just before it all fell apart, his family helped me get a job at a day care as a cook. I love to bake cakes and cookies, but cooking all day every day for twenty to thirty little children was not my dream job. I also knew I did not want to leave my boys all day every day. I did not want to have someone else raise them, so I took the job, and I was able to have them with me. I had been a stay-at-home mom for the past seven years, and I did not want to miss anything the boys did. It really wasn't a tough job; I just do not like washing dishes all the time. I loved the relationships I had with my coworkers. We all got along most of the time. They have been a true blessing to me and my family. I began working at Tykes Early Childhood Development Center on September 16, 2002, which was owned by a company called REIC Laboratory. This company analyzed soil and water samples for other companies. The child-care facility started so their employees would have a place for their children to stay while they worked. In the kitchen, I cooked breakfast and lunch daily. I also made snacks for the afternoon. I would leave around three fifteen and pick up the school-age children off the bus and then completed my day. This was my day, not real interesting until a few weeks into it.

The List

It began like any other day cooking breakfast; two guys carrying a cooler knocked on the kitchen door and asked if they could have some ice. They worked in the lab, and their samples were needed to be kept on ice. I welcomed them into the kitchen, told them to help themselves, and returned preparing breakfast. Not much was said, and they left. Their faces became familiar, but I did not know their names. Most days the guys would stop in. Sometimes it would be early, and other times it would be late. When they didn't show up, I would wonder where they were. One day they showed up just as breakfast was over. We had some food left, so I offered it to them. That was all it took because they started showing up every day just as breakfast was over. They were like vultures. They made sure the leftovers were not wasted. I still did not know their names. I became interested in the guy with a gray circle patch of hair. I would think about him during the day and wonder if he was going to need more ice. I would think of him as my iceman. Boy, is he cute! But I have two boys, and he may be dating someone, or he could even be married. Who says he was even interested? I just don't know; was I ready to date again? I will just give it some time.

In early October, I decided to attend a Women of Faith conference with my mom and a few other ladies. We had a wonderful time. I remember Thelma Wells, one of the speakers, talking about being "anxious for *nothing*, *no* thing."

> Rejoice in the Lord always: and again I say, Rejoice. Let your moderation be known to all men. The Lord is at hand. Be careful for nothing; but in everything by prayer and supplication, with thanksgiving, let your requests be known unto God. And the peace of God, which passeth all understanding, shall keep your hearts and minds through Christ Jesus. Finally, brethren, whatsoever things are true, whatsoever things are honest, whatsoever things are just, whatsoever things are pure, whatsoever things are lovely, whatsoever things are of good report, if there be any virtue and if there is any praise, think on these things. Those things, which ye have both learned, and received, and heard, and seen in me, do: and the God of peace shall be with you. But I rejoiced in the Lord greatly, that now at the last your care of me hath flourished again; wherein ye were also careful, but ye lacked opportunity. Not that I speak in respect of want, for I have learned, in whatsoever state I am, *therewith* to be content. I know both how to be abased, and I know how to

abound: every where and in all things I instructed both to be full and to be hungry, both to abound and to suffer need. I can do all things through Christ which strengtheneth me.

Philippians 4:4–13

These words hit home. I had been at my lowest, and I knew the Lord could bring me through. Her words were talking directly to me from God. Boy, did it hit me like a ton of bricks, and I knew from that point on my life would forever be changed.

I do not remember much more about that weekend, but I do remember going back to my apartment and giving my whole self to the Lord to use me for his glory. I had been saved as a child, and as any child, I would stray from time to time, but this time I was grown and knew he was all I had, and he would listen no matter how bad I had been. God was there for me. Don't get me wrong, my family has always been there for me, but I needed something more. I had made a mess of my life, and the only one to fix it would be my Lord and Savior. I prayed a lot and knew I had made poor choices in my life, so giving everything over to God was all I knew to do. In doing this, I began a new way of doing things. First, I would be anxious for nothing. Let my life go fast or slow—whichever the Lord wanted—and I would be patient. Patience was definitely a hard concept for me. Usually when I wanted something, I would pursue it until I achieved it. Patience was my first lesson on listening to God and determining what he wanted for me. Next, I realized I needed to pray about every situation no matter how big or small it was. I would need to ask what God thought and then wait for an answer. Here is that patience thing again. I did not make a lot of money working at the child-care center, so money was tight, but I knew if I trusted that God would provide, I needed not be anxious or worried. When the time would come, the money would be there. Remember, I was in a process of learning to trust my whole life to God. I was always able to make my rent and pay my other bills, and we always had enough food to eat. God was providing without me having to ask anyone for help. It was amazing. This is the way I live my life.

Every evening I would read Philippians 4 from beginning to end and was learning something new each time I read it. I realized I could make all my requests known to God; I was beginning to feel a little lonely, so I requested that God send me someone of his choosing. I obviously did not make wise decisions about the guys I went out with, so I knew if God picked him for me, I could not go wrong. I wondered how I would know if he was the one that God sent. I knew I could make a detailed list of what I would like my future husband to be. Beginning the list was not hard; I knew if it was to work, he would have to be a Christian and have the same beliefs as I did. This was my first criteria. Second, he will have to love children, no exceptions; my boys, Brandon and Ryan, were too important to me. If someone did not like children, especially mine, there was no way it would work. Third, he could not have any children of his own. Some may think this is a little selfish, but I don't care. I knew God would provide this, or he would not be the one. I knew that if he loved my children first before he experienced loving his own, then he would always have a special place in his heart for them even after the birth of his children. Next, he could not have a crazy ex-girlfriend or wife because they usually try to cause trouble. This could also be considered selfish, but this is what I wanted. This request went hand in hand with criteria number 5: he could not have ever been married. My future husband had to be courteous; I wanted to feel special, like a princess. I wanted someone to open doors for me and do the little things that so many guys do not do. Finally, he could not try anything on our first date—kiss or anything else. I just wanted him to hold my hand—nothing more. And now, I had my list, and it was all the things I felt were important to me. I wondered how I would know that he is the one. I wanted no doubt in my mind, so I needed one more criteria. I really needed to think this through because it had to be an unusual act! I had it. As he is leaving the date, he has to ask me if he can call me instead of "I will give you a call sometime." He will have to ask me if it is all right for him to call me. In my experience, no guy had ever done this. They would always say, "Hey, I'll give you a call," so this was the clincher. If he does this silly little thing, I know he was sent by God.

Meeting Biscuit Lady

In late summer of 2002, my friend and coworker Tom told me that he was going to be dealing with a new method of analysis. Working at an environmental testing lab, there were different methods and analysis for different materials. This new method involved testing chicken droppings, which required ice for the method of analysis. We had no source for ice in our lab. Our boss, the owner of the company, also owned a child day-care center located in the building behind the lab. At this day-care, they had an ice-making machine. Tom informed me that he would need my help carrying the cooler full of ice from the day care to the lab every day for a while. The chicken droppings arrived at the lab, and off we went to get the ice from the day care. We had always considered the day care employees coworkers; many of the lab employees had children who attended the child-care center. Lab employees and day care employees often socialized with one another at company picnics and Christmas parties, so we knew nearly everyone who worked at the day care.

The first day Tom and I retrieved ice, we went into the day care and asked one of the managers if it was all right to get some ice; it was, so we then proceeded into the kitchen where the ice machine was located. In the kitchen was a person neither Tom nor I knew. I was not sure if she was a visitor or a new employee. The next day, she was working in the kitchen again, so I knew she must be a new employee. We made regular visits to the day care center. One day we arrived just as breakfast for the children was over. The curly, brown-haired cook, who we did not know, offered Tom and I some of the leftovers. Of course we took her up on it. Being a pair of opportunistic individuals, Tom and I timed our regular visits to the day care center just as breakfast was ending for the children. Every day, Mondays through Fridays, we got ice around 8:45 a.m. for the chicken-poop samples. We would fill up the cooler, eat some leftovers, then talk to the curly, brown-haired cook, and return to the lab. By this time, we had given her the name Biscuit Girl (because biscuits were our favorite), and we did not know her real name. One of those early days of getting ice, I made it a point to look at the Biscuit Girl's left-hand ring finger. No ring, I wondered if she was single, or if she just took her ring off to cook.

The ice trips continued, and the conversations with the Biscuit Girl grew friendlier. I began to notice that the Biscuit Girl tended to look my direction a lot during our "breakfast" conversations. One day I asked her if she had a child who attended the day care. She replied that she had two children there. This would have turned a lot of guys that I knew off, but it really did not faze me. My previous dating experience was with a woman who also had two children, so her answer did not bother me.

Late summer turned to autumn, and by now it was mid-October. It was around this time that the Biscuit Girl did something I'll never forget. We showed up one morning to get ice, and she asked if we wanted a biscuit. Of course we did; biscuits were our favorite. She told Tom to go ahead to get one, then she turned, and she handed my biscuit to me. The look on her face and the smile she had let me know that she must like something about me. I know it may not seem like much to you, but to me, I will never forget her face at that moment. That moment I knew I wanted to ask her out for a date, but I wondered how when every day when I saw her, Tom was with me. After all, it was his chicken-poop samples we had to get the ice for. Calling her was a problem because I worked in a crowded area of the lab, and I did not want to embarrass myself in front of my coworkers. They could be rather ruthless and brutal, especially if they overheard me asking someone out over the phone. Also, I did not know her home phone number or her cell number. Most importantly, I still did not know her name! It wasn't but a day or so later that one of my coworkers from the lab, Beth, stopped me in the hall and informed me that someone who worked at the day care liked me. Beth had children who attended the day care and was told this information by one of the Biscuit Girl's coworkers. I knew exactly who she was referring to, but I went ahead and asked Beth who she was talking about. She said the cook. I replied that I was very interested, but there was a problem. I did not know the cooks name. Beth said she would find out for me.

On the morning of Friday October 25, 2002, Beth handed me a yellow Post-It note that said, "Her name is Tonya Laxton; she is 27 with two children." The day care phone number was also in the note. I already knew the phone number to the day care, but the problem was finding the right time and place to call her. I decided that the best time to call was at lunch. All of my coworkers would be out of the work area, and then I could feel free to ask her out without my coworkers heckling me. My plan worked. I skipped lunch; since no one was at our work station, I gave the Biscuit Girl a call. She was not there. Her boss said she just left to run an errand and would be back in a half an hour or so. Great, I thought, now I would need to call her with my coworkers back in our portion of the lab. Time went by, I was getting anxious, finally around two thirty or so, I found myself by the phone all alone, so I called up the Biscuit Girl, Tonya. I knew I did not want to push my luck, be forward, and ask her out to dinner. I was going to keep it simple. I called the number, and a voice answered on the other end; I asked to speak to Tonya.

The voice said, "This is she." I told her who I was; she knew. "I was wondering if you would like to maybe go and have a cup of coffee with me or something. Although I don't drink coffee, I could find something to drink." She said yes; needless to say, I was thrilled. This extremely cute, curly- and brown-haired lady, who we called the Biscuit Girl, was going to go out with me. We made plans for Saturday night because that night, Friday, she had to be a clown for a kid's birthday party. (Tonya is a clown; she does parties for kids, paints faces, makes balloon animals, etc.) After her clown party was over, I called her on her cell phone, and we talked until she arrived home. We got off the phone, and I was looking forward for the next night.

Meeting Iceman

This day began a little differently; a few days before, I had started asking if anyone knew the cute guy, also known as My Iceman. None of the ladies I worked with knew him, but Susie told me she would find out so that I would quit talking about him and get my mind on work. When I arrived, there was a little yellow sticky note on the dishwasher.

I thought, *What could this be? I am going to hurt Susie. What has she done?*

The note read, "Greg Mills, single, assistant golf coach SS High School."

I panicked. *Oh no, has he came to get ice yet this morning? I hope he has not. I know that some days they get in here early, and then come back when breakfast is over.*

I was so embarrassed. My mind filled with questions. *What if he saw this? What will I say? Do I just play it off as just needing to know his name? What if he is not interested, I would never be able to face him again.* "Susie!" I yelled. "What have you done? Are you crazy!"

Her thoughts were, "Well, that is the first place you go to in the mornings to turn on the dishwasher, so it will be heated up by the time breakfast is over. He usually comes after breakfast." Okay, she was forgiven. I have a name: Greg Mills. Aw, how sweet, and he is single, a major plus.

About a week before all this, My Iceman and I were standing in front of the stove talking; he casually asked me, "So, do you have a kid here?"

And of course I let him know. "Yes, I have two boys; they are three and four."

"Oh wow, two," he replied sounding surprised; he must have been interested. Now I'm not so sure. Two kids, he probably thought. The look on his face spoke for itself. I told Susie and Maudee that if there was a chance, it was no longer a possibility. I still needed to know his name, so Susie took care of that for me. Now remember, all things are possible if the Lord is in control. I was starting to get the hang of this patience thing; it was not so bad. Since Susie found out his name from Beth, who worked with Greg at the lab, I was certain he knew someone was interested in him. I was certain she and Susie would now try to play matchmakers.

I thought, *If he finds out it is me, he will probably remember our conversation the week before about my boys. He will not want to go out, so I am not going to get my hopes up so then I won't be disappointed.*

Beth seemed to think he was interested, so she asked me if I would have my boys that weekend. It just so happened that they were going to be with their dad, but I had a clown party on Friday. It would have to be Saturday or nothing, and this was only if he asked me out. Will he or won't he? I guess I will have to wait.

On October 25, 2002, Beth said that Greg was going to call me. I waited and waited and waited. I had to leave and run to the store. *Great! Watch, he will call when I am gone. Be anxious for nothing, remember.*

Guess what? You guessed it. He called about a minute or so after I left for the store. Susie told him to call back in about a half hour. So I waited and waited and waited again. I thought, *Is he ever going to call me back?*

The phone rang; it was for me. My heart was pounding almost as if it would come out of my chest. It was him.

"Hello! Hey, sorry I missed your call earlier; they needed me to run to the store," I said.

"I was wondering if you would like to maybe go and have a cup of coffee with me or something. Although I don't drink coffee, I could find something to drink," Greg said.

Okay, now this was a new one for me. He just wanted to get some coffee. Why wouldn't he ask me to dinner or something, hmm?

"Sure, that would be great," I said. "My boys will be gone for the weekend, so, yea, I could; although tonight would not be good. I have to be in Bluefield to be a clown at a kid's birthday party."

My Iceman, I mean Greg, said, "Well, tomorrow would be better for me too because I am supposed to be at a ball game this evening."

"So tomorrow it is," I replied. "I will call you on my way back from the party this evening when I have service, and we can figure out what time and where."

"Okay, great." And the call ended. I felt like a little schoolgirl going out on my first date ever. What would I wear? Will my clown makeup stain my face? Off to the clown party, I can't wait till it is over, and we can talk again.

As I headed back to the apartment, Greg and I talked on the phone, the date was set, we were going out to dinner at Applebee's restaurant in Beckley, which will be wonderful. Saturday October 26, 2002 will change our lives forever. I will have to remember my pact with God and trust him to give me the words to find out all I need to know and to see if Greg will be approved for a second date.

I needed a new outfit for a new beginning, so off to the mall I went. I found a nice pair of slate-gray slacks and an eggplant, ribbed, long-sleeve shirt at New York & Company.

This will do, I thought.

I am not big on shopping. My idea of shopping is go in, get something, and get out of there fast. I asked my mom to stop by to see if the outfit I purchased looked good and to make sure my hair and makeup were all right. I was so nervous, I had never been nervous on a first date, so I thought, *Why am I so nervous?* I had butterflies in my stomach. *What is wrong with me?*

I hurried my mom out the door as I didn't want her to be there when he got there. She touched up my hair, and off she went. Shortly after my mom left, there was a knock on my door. It was Greg. He walked me to the passenger side of the car and opened the door for me.

I thought, *One rule down, seven more to go.* Now we were off to dinner.

At Applebee's, Greg got out of the car and came around to open my door for me to get out. We had to wait for a few minutes before they found a table for us. We looked at the photographs in the entryway. Many of them were of my old classmates at Woodrow Wilson High School, so we talked a bit about them. The host took us to our table—the first, two-seated booth to the left of the front door.

The Date

Although we do not remember what we ate, we do remember we had a wonderful time. We engaged in deep conversation, finding out about each other's likes and dislikes, as well as who we were. Our date at Applebee's will be one we'll never forget. We had a lot we needed to find out about each other, things we needed to know to see if we would even have a second date. We both attended church and were of the Baptist faith. That was a plus. I also discovered that he enjoyed working with kids but has none of his own. Theses were the two most important criteria on my list. I checked number 2 and 3 off the list. I also crossed off number 6 because he really made me feel special. He opened the doors for me; he still had no clue he was being tested and was going to have to pass it to get a second date. With four down, there were still four more items on the list.

"So, have you ever been married?" I asked him.

"No," he replied.

"Great! No crazy exes then? Including girl friends?" I said jokingly, but I needed to know.

"No, I have not been that serious with anyone," Greg said.
Six down now, only two more to go. Will he pass?

We talked for three hours at Applebee's, and the waiter kept coming to our table to see if we needed anything else. We did not; we decided the waiter needed the table free, so we left.

I remembered that I was supposed to make muffins for Sunday school; I asked Greg if he cared to stop by my parents' home to pick up their muffin pans so I would not have to go back out after he took me home. I know Greg thought, *What is she doing? Why does she want me to meet her parents already? That is kind of weird.*

We stopped by my parents' home, and then off to the apartment we went. Our conversations continued at the apartment for two more hours. He was such a gentleman; he did not even try to hold my hand. Awesome, only one more item on the list. We could have talked for hours, but we were both tired and had church early in the morning, so Greg decided it was time to leave for the evening. My apartment door was hard to shut, so when he pulled it shut, it did not close all the way. He then peeked his head back in the apartment and said one last thing I will never forget. "Hey, would you care if I give you a call sometime?"

I could not believe it. No guy had ever asked me this, or could I have been hearing things? No, he said it! My heart leapt for joy. He was the one God had picked for me, and I have finally found him. I replied, "Sure, anytime." Greg left, and the happy dance began.

We went out numerous times after the first date, we cannot recall every detail, but we both knew one thing: we really enjoyed each other's company. The boys grew fond of Greg during this time, and he grew fond of them. They enjoyed playing games, going to parks, and just having fun. As we grew closer, Greg wanted me to meet his parents; at the time I did not realize the significance of this, so around Thanksgiving, he arranged a time for us to get together. We went over to his mom's house one evening, and I remember how nervous I was. I never got nervous about meeting anyone, but this was different I so wanted her to like me. The evening went well. We sat around watching television with them and had wonderful conversations. After we left, I remember asking Greg if his mom liked his other girlfriends, and he proceeded to tell me that she only met a couple of them. He normally didn't let his parents to meet the girls he took out.

Wow! I thought. *He must like me a lot.* A week or so later, we went out to dinner with his dad and his dad's wife at the Rio Grande Mexican Restaurant. The dinner went well. We talked a bit, and we enjoyed the evening.

Sometime around Christmas, Greg and I were talking about our relationship. We both noticed this relationship was different than any relationship either one of us had ever had. It seemed God had placed us in the right place at the right time.

Greg never liked chemistry in school and could not understand why, until now, that he got the job at the lab.

I didn't understand how I got the job at the day care cooking when I had a degree in drafting and design.

The more we talked about it, the more he was convinced that our relationship had to be God sent. I knew it because of my list, but he knew nothing of it. Now is the time to spill the beans. "Greg, I know God put us together," I said. "I have known since the first date."

"How did you know this?" he asked.

"Well, you are going to think this is crazy, but you had to pass a list of criteria on the first date," I exclaimed.

"What? A list. Well, what was on the list? Did I pass?" he said.

"Well duh, you are here, aren't you?" I said a little sarcastically.

He said, "I guess so! So what was this list about?"

"You had to pass eight criteria before I would continue to go out with you," I said.

"Oh really, so what were they?" Greg wanted to know.

I proceeded to tell him the criteria on my list, leaving out the stupid one the asking-to-call-me part.

"That is only seven, what was the eighth one?" Greg wanted to know.

"Oh, it is just stupid," I said. "It doesn't matter, you passed, and that is what is important."

After going back and forth a few times, I decided to tell Greg the eighth one. "Okay, okay," I said. "I will tell you. You are probably gonna laugh and think I am crazy, but I knew if you did this, I would have no doubt you were sent to me from God. You had to ask if you could call me, not just say, 'I'll give you a call sometime.'"

The room was silent for what seemed like an eternity, and Greg's face just had this weird look on it. Then he said, "I have never asked to call any girl. I have always said, 'Hey, I'll give you a call sometime.'"

Whoa! We were both stunned. Silence returned while we thought about everything. Could this be a relationship truly heaven-sent?

The Surprise

Every way of a man is right in his own eyes: But the LORD pondereth the hearts.

Proverbs 21:2

Following the Lord's way is not always easy, and many times we will fail. The Lord looks at our heart and soul, and he knows who we truly are, making our crooked paths straight. We are far from perfect, but we choose to follow the ways of God, and he has brought us through many trials so that we may grow and rely on him always.

April 2003 was a month we will never forget. I had surgery on my knee because of a snow-skiing accident in January. We were planning a trip to watch the Los Angeles Dodgers play the Pittsburgh Pirates at Pittsburgh. The games were scheduled for April 25, 26, and 27. Little did Tonya know, my plans were to propose to her at the game across the message board, but with the unexpected surgery, I did not get this worked out. I would postpone it to our first year anniversary. She would like that.

We were both getting anxious for the last weekend in April, but Tonya wasn't feeling well; in the spring, her allergies are pretty bad.

Tonya's Thoughts

Before we left, I needed to go to the doctor to get some medicine, or I was going to be miserable the whole trip. I also did not want it turning into a sinus infection, so on Thursday, I stopped by Doctors' Immedicare to get the medication I needed. That night I had a dream. Most people who know me well know that when I have a dream, it may not be just a dream. Many times, they will come true. I woke up quite scared. *What was I to do? I needed to take a test. Oh no! Do I wait till after this weekend? I will just take the test. It is probably nothing.* I guess you figured out my dream—well, at least what it consisted of. You see, each time I have had this particular dream, I got a special gift after about nine months. This was the third dream of this nature. I bought a test and decided to take it before I showered, and I would check it afterward. All right, was the dream for real or just a warning? I looked at the test— nothing, just one line. O*kay, I will get ready and check it one more time before I leave for work.* Oh my! What is this? Is that a faint line in the result box? I think it is. Oh no, maybe it is where I waited to read it? It can't be right? Can it?

I went to work really early so I could get everything done by lunch, clean up the dishes, and then leave for our trip. Susie knew right away that something was up. She knew we were going on the trip, but I had everything ready by 8:00 a.m.; breakfast and lunch were out and just needed heating up. The kitchen was clean, and breakfast was waiting on all the kids to arrive. This never happened, so Susie could see right through me.

"What's up?" Susie said.

"Oh nothing, I am just excited for our trip," I said. Susie wasn't buying it; I could tell. "Well, I had this dream—"

"Oh, I thought you were going to tell me you are pregnant or something!" exclaimed Susie.

"Well, you didn't hear the rest of the story. I had a dream, and with my experience with this particular dream, I knew it could be true and not just a dream. I dreamed I was in a delivery room having a baby," I said

Susie said, "Well, it was just a dream, right?"

"I wasn't so sure, so I took a test, and the result window had a faint line in it, but it was just a cheap test, so it may have been a defective one!" I explained.

"I am going to the store right now and get you a good one. I'll be right back," Susie told me.

I finished serving breakfast, and after the children returned to their classes, I went to take the test Susie got for me. In the mean time, Maudee arrived and sensed something was up, so Susie decided to tell her. The three of us were hovering over this test. Looking back, it was kind of funny, but at the time we were all scared to death.

"I see two lines, but one is too light," Susie said.

Maudee agreed, "It should be darker."

So we got the instructions out and read through them. It stated if there are two lines, it is positive even if one line is lighter than the other. Susie handed me the second test in the box and told me to go and take it. Again, we waited, hovering over this test. The results were in. I was pregnant, and what was I going to do? Maudee, Susie, and I debated. "Should Greg know before the trip, during the trip, or after the trip?" This was a hard question. I definitely did not want to ruin his trip by him worrying the entire time, but I did not want him upset at me for not telling him.

"I wouldn't tell him," Maudee said.

"I think you should tell him before you leave," Susie said.

I knew if I told him before, we wouldn't be going, but we all agreed that I would not tell him while he was driving.

It was almost time to leave, and knowing what we did, I could not take any more of my medicine for my allergies, so I stuck it in the filing cabinet along with the pregnancy tests. I waited for Greg to pick me up, and off we went on our trip to Pittsburgh, Pennsylvania. My mind was wondering the entire trip, but Greg did not realize anything was wrong. My allergies were really acting up, constant sneezing, itchy watery eyes, the works. Greg asked me if I had taken my medicine, so knowing I had left it at Tykes, I said, "Oh no, I left it at Tykes in the filing cabinet [not lying]. I will be okay."

Greg said, "That isn't good. We can stop and get you some over-the-counter stuff after we get there."

"Okay" I said.

We arrived at the stadium and were filled with excitement. We both love baseball, and to see it live is awesome. The game was great, and the food was good and greasy. It was late, so after the game, we went to the hotel and went to bed. We had forgotten to get me any medicine. *Thank goodness*, I thought. We got up early and went to breakfast, excited for the day ahead. While at the game, I snuck away from Greg for a few minutes to look for something for a baby outfit. When I tell him, I wanted to have something to give him from the game. Greg's team is the Dodgers, but we were at Pittsburgh, so they did not have anything but Pirate stuff. I found this cute little ball outfit with the *P* logo on it. Not knowing if the baby would be a boy or girl, I had to get something that could be for either. Heading back to our seats, I stuffed it in my bib overalls so he wouldn't ask me what I bought. What a wonderful day we had. Again we can't remember all the details, but we knew one thing that we really loved each other and enjoyed spending this time together. On our way back to the hotel, Greg stopped and got me some medicine. Do I just act like I take it, or do I tell him? This was Saturday night, then we had one more game to go to on Sunday, and we would head home afterward. Greg gave me the medicine, and I decided to tell him I couldn't take it. Greg asked, "Why can't you take it? Is there a medical condition?"

So I said, "Kind of." Well, this got the wheels turning in his head, and he was trying to think of a medical condition that wouldn't allow this type of medicine. He was clueless. I got out the gift I had purchased and handed it to him without saying anything; he opened it and said, "Is this for Abigail? She is my niece who was born in October."

I said, "No, just think about it for a minute." Then it hit him like a ton of bricks. He sat down on the side of the bed rubbing his goatee and shaking his head; I'll let him tell you the rest of that story.

Greg's Thoughts

The news that Tonya gave me that night at the hotel hit me like a ton of bricks. I was stunned, scared, and unsure of what was going to happen. I had always wanted a child, but this news was sudden and unexpected. I am the type of person who likes to be in control of every situation. For the first time, in a long time, I was not in control of what was happening. We were in Pittsburgh watching baseball games, Friday and Saturday nights; we were not sure if we were going to Sunday's game. After the news I received from Tonya on Saturday, there was no way I could sit still and watch a baseball game Sunday afternoon. We decided to head on home. The drive home from Pittsburgh was about three and a half hours, and it was an unusual experience, I might add. I went through so many emotions in that short period of time. There were periods of time we talked about our future, and then there were other times of complete silence. We talked about marriage and informing our relatives about the situation. We arrived back at Tonya's place that evening, and we decided the next day we must tell our loved ones of the news I received the night before.

I had known for a while now that I would ask Tonya, sooner or later, to be my wife. However, with the events we just described, the time for asking was now. Obviously, I did not have time to prepare or buy a ring or anything, but the time was now. We were sitting on her couch talking. She got up and went to the kitchen for something to drink, and when she walked back to the couch, I got down on one knee and asked her to marry me. I realized this was not very romantic, but the news of her pregnancy was stunning. We felt the best course of action was to handle these matters quickly. I cannot remember much of what I said. The one thing I do remember clearly about that moment was the smile Tonya had on her face while I was kneeling in front of her. This was all meant to be.

The next day was Monday, and we both had to be back at work; however, we knew this was the day we had to tell our parents and relatives that Tonya was pregnant and that we were going to get married on the weekend. Let me say, this was the most nervous I have ever been. Looking back, I should not have been so nervous. We were both adults, I was thirty-two, and Tonya was twenty-eight; however, at that time I felt like we were teenagers having to face our parents with this startling news.

We decided to tell my mom the news first. We met her for lunch, and immediately she knew something was going on. When we all sat down to eat, Mom said, "So, guys, what's up?" We told her the whole situation, Tonya's pregnancy and our plans to marry each other the following weekend. Mom was excited that she was finally going to be a grandmother. Once lunch was over, we returned to work, still nervous because we would tell the rest of our parents that evening. After work, Tonya and I went to her parents' house to inform them of the news, and they handled it well too. Finally, we had to tell my dad. This was when I was most nervous. I decided the best way to inform him was to dive straight in and tell him, not to wait around with small talk or conversation. His reaction was much like mine when he heard the news. I can only describe it as stunned silence. The hard part was over, and now we just had to wait until Friday when we were going to be married.

Whirlwind

Trust in the LORD with all thine heart; and lean
not unto thine own understanding. In all thy ways
acknowledge him, and he shall direct thy paths.

Proverbs 3:5–6

May 2, 2003, was a special day. We chose this day because it
was the first weekend after the big news, and we wanted to
make everything right. We did not realize it was already a
special day, the day Tonya was saved twenty years before. She
figured this out in the winter of 2010 when she ran across
her Bible that was given to her when she was baptized.

We did not want a big wedding and decided to just go
off and get married, instead of wasting money we did not
have. We chose Pearisburg, Virginia, and were married
by Suzie Dobson (not Susie from Tykes), outside with a
beautiful view of the mountains. It was quick and sweet
and what we both wanted. We went on our honeymoon to
Alderson, West Virginia, where Tonya's grandparents have
an old farmhouse they call the Farm. Just before we got

there, a small tornado had went through a nearby town, Ronceverte, and knocked out the power in parts of three counties. We had a nice time, going on walks, going on a drive, and spending time together. It was just the two of us, Mr. and Mrs. Gregory Lee Mills. On June 14, 2003, we decided to have a reception to celebrate our marriage with our families, which turned out quite nice. My family who did not get to make it to the reception would soon get to meet my new family, a wife and two young sons. They met the family at the Wiley Cullop Family Reunion, held in Summers County, West Virginia, the last weekend in June each year. Tonya would get to meet fifteen different families, all are my mom's brothers' and sisters' children and grandchildren. She did not know what to expect. I will let her share how she felt.

***

Tonya's Thoughts

I must say it was very surprising to see this many people all directly related to Greg, his aunts, uncles, first cousins, second cousins, and a few third cousins; a lot of people and I did not know what to expect. They all welcomed me and my boys with open arms, I do not remember a lot of the details, but I do remember thinking, *Wow!*

One conversation I do remember was sitting with Greg's cousin Stephanie, we clicked right away, and I felt I had known her all my life. We were sitting on a step to one of the cabins, and she looked at Greg and said, "So what's the scandal this year? Who and what is everyone talking about? What has happened since last reunion?' Then she realized what she said and looked straight at Greg and said, "Oh yeah, you are!" We all busted out laughing and told her our story. The reunion is a special time that we all enjoy and for me, and my boys we have always fit right in like it has always been.

As you can see, our lives had been a whirlwind, and it was only beginning. We knew we needed to get a house soon so we could settle in before the little one arrived. We started looking and found a nice three-bedroom, one-and-three-fourths bath, red, brick, raised ranch, located in a little community called Midway. We gave a full-price offer and would soon get our new home. Somewhere in the midst of all this, I wanted to share something Ryan said that was cute. When we got married, Brandon was almost five, and Ryan was almost four, and they knew we were now a family but did not understand much about things. They didn't understand why Greg slept in the bed with Mommy now and things of that sort, but one thing Ryan seemed to know was that when people got married, they needed to have a baby, if he only knew. One day we sat the boys down and told them we would be having a baby around the first of the year, after Christmas, and Ryan stood up and said, "See, I told you—that's what happens when you get married. You have a baby!"

Greg and I just started laughing and said, "You did tell us that, didn't you?"

He said, "Yep!" with a big smile on his face and then sat down; he was so proud.

We would soon get to find out what we were having and wanted to involve Brandon and Ryan in everything so they would feel we were a real family. We decided to take them along to the ultrasound, but we had to have a little talk before we went in because Brandon wanted a girl, and Ryan wanted a boy. We knew it would be either or, but not both so we needed to prepare them. We proceeded to tell them that God has given us this baby, and we need to be happy whether it is a boy or girl. We told them God would give us what we needed.

While we were in the room with the baby on the screen, Brandon looked at it and said, "Well, it looks like it is an alligator, not a baby!" with a little bit of attitude. What he saw was the baby's leg bent at the knee so it did look like an alligator's mouth. We all started laughing, and the time came when the technician could tell. She told us, "It's a boy!"

When we returned to the car, Brandon looked at me and said, "Why did God think we needed another boy!"

We told him, "Because he wanted you and Ryan to be able to teach him lots of things you know how to do, like play baseball and stuff like that."

Brandon said, "Okay." And that was the end of that. We later realized that he was wanting a little sister because little brothers are the same size as him, but little girls are tiny, and he could hold them. Brandon and Ryan are a year and eighteen days apart, and Brandon did not remember Ryan being little; it is amazing how kids think.

Greg's Thoughts

When the calendar year of 2003 began, I was a single guy with very little responsibility. By the time the year was ending, I was married with a new family, a new house, and a new baby almost here. The year was hectic, frantic, and wonderful; it ended with one of the greatest joys of my life. By Christmas, Tonya was nearly ready to give birth to our baby. We already knew that the child was going to be a boy, and we were going to name him Matthew. On the night of December 28, 2003, Tonya was feeling bad and, being the experienced mother that she is, informed me that we needed to go to the hospital. I was scared and excited all at the same time and knew that my firstborn would be here soon. At 8:00 a.m. December 29, 2003, Tonya was in full labor, and at 8:54 a.m., I saw for the first time my beautiful son. I'll never forget all the joy and emotions that came over me at that time. Matthew was here, and I was a dad. What a way to cap off a whirlwind year.

When 2004 began, we were a family of five living in a new house. Tonya and I realized that we needed more income to support our family and our new home. The job at the lab was fine for a single guy, but now with five mouths to feed, we needed more money. Two years earlier, just before I met Tonya, I had looked into a master's program through Marshall University where I could enter grad school and receive a teaching certificate with a master's degree. I let that opportunity pass at that time; however, fast-forward two years, this was an option for us to take. After Tonya and I had many conversations about this move and much prayer concerning this issue, I enrolled at Marshall grad school in the fall of 2004 and began the process of getting a teaching certificate and master's degree. My goal going in was to complete this program in two years; it was going to be tough, working during the day to support my new family and taking classes in the evening, but it was possible. Remember, with God all things are possible; I also had the loving support of Tonya.

My advisor at Marshall suggested letting it take three years to complete the program, but this was not an option, it had to be finished in two years. After much work and many miles traveled, I began my studies in August 2004 and graduated in May, 2006, with a master's degree and a teaching certificate. God is good!

I must fill you in on some events that took place between August 2004 and May 2006. During this two-year process of going back to school, I quit my job at the lab in February 2005 and began substitute teaching for the rest of that school year. Then for the 2005–2006 school year, I received a long-term substitute teaching position at Independence High School, teaching history for the entire school year. I began the 2006–2007 school year with a permanent teaching position; I was certified as a teacher at the same school I had the long-term substitute position.

Even though teaching is not a highly lucrative profession, it did allow us to make more money and more importantly spend more time with my family. Why teaching, you may ask? The job at the lab wasn't as glamorous as it may seem. It was less pay, and I had gone as high up the ladder there as I possibly could. So, why teaching? Well, my father had made a career in the teaching profession. It paid the bills for his family when I was growing up, and he is my example and the one I look up to. With the help of two very important individuals, first, the Lord and then my wife, Tonya, I had successfully changed professions.

During the two years of grad school, Tonya and I had discussed the possibility of adding another member to our family. We concluded that we would try to add another child to our home. Personally, I wanted another child to call my own, and Tonya had always wanted a little girl (up to this point she had three children, all boys). At some point, I'm not sure when during the period between the end of 2004 and the beginning of 2005 we thought Tonya had become pregnant. She was sure that she was. She had all the "symptoms," and she even took a pregnancy test, which was positive. We began telling people that we were expecting up until she went to the doctor to find out we were not. We are unsure of what happened, but looking back on the situation, it was not in God's plan to have a child at that time. While waiting on God, Tonya had a real heart to heart with God on how she wanted a little girl. One day we were talking with my grandmother, and the topic of having another child was brought up. I thought three children would be plenty, but Tonya informed all of us that she talked to God, and she would be having a little girl. She also informed me that I had nothing to do with it. We all began to laugh, including Tonya, but she really had her heart set on a little girl. As 2005 moved on, I was in the midst of my schooling, and she finally became pregnant. After continually trying, we were going to add a sixth member to our family. The due date was sometime in May 2006. Just to show you how God's timing is always right, my official graduation date for the master's degree program at Marshall was May 6, 2006 and our precious little princess, Sarah Ann, was born on May 8, 2006. God knows best! Tonya had gotten the little girl she had always dreamed of, and I had the second child

I had longed for. The Lord has blessed us more than we had ever imagined, and looking back on the period from 2003 to 2006, I believe God was preparing us for what was about to happen in 2008.

The Move

I waited patiently for the LORD; and he inclined unto me, and heard my cry.

Psalm 40:1

Patience, I believe, is one of the hardest things to learn but is truly one of the best things to learn. Being patient and waiting on the Lord is sweet. In his timing, you will have the greatest reward. In the past nine years, I have struggled with being patient, and looking back, things always fell apart when I did it in my timing. Waiting on God produces different results, awesome results.

By 2007, we were out growing our Midway home and were considering adding on to it. After talking with a few contractors on the cost of adding a couple more rooms, I discovered it was not going to be an option; the cost was way too high. We began praying that if it be the Lord's will, let it be done, but we were in need of a larger home. We looked into building a house, and it would be expensive, especially if we had to purchase land. Tonya's parents had some land they were going to sign over to us, and we could build on it, but those plans fell through. The state needed that particular piece of property to make an access road to the Veterans Hospital; obviously this was not God's plan for us. We knew that we needed to get our finances in order so that God could bless us, so in December 2007, Tonya ran across a book *The Total Money Makeover* by Dave Ramsey. Our company was promoting this particular book to help people get out of debt, and they had a read-a-thon set to start in January 2008. Tonya was bound and determined to become financially free as God intends everyone to be. Being much in prayer, Tonya set some goals to have most everything paid off by May 2008; we did not know how we were going to do this, but with the Lord's help, we knew we could achieve this. Looking at all we owed, most people would have given up right then and would have taken the bankruptcy way, but knowing that is not what would be pleasing to God, we knew there had to be another way. It may take longer, but setting a budget would be the first step, a hard one but a must. Looking at our income versus our debt, it looked impossible to swim out; we'll give you a quick overview of what we can remember: mortgage left to be paid, $56,000; van payoff, $12,500; student loan, $8,000; credit cards, $7,000. For our other debts, Tonya's parents took over, but we want to repay $15,550. This doesn't include any regularly occurring bills such as utility, medical, living expenses; with $99,050 debt, all I knew to say was *ugh*! Prayer, prayer, and more prayer—how could we possibly get out of this financial mess? "Cast thy burden upon the LORD, and he shall sustain thee" (Psalm 55:22, KJV). This is what we did, cast our burden on the Lord so he would take care of the mess for us, and let me say how amazingly he did this. We give him all the glory!

Bringing in around $40,000 of income per year, we could not see how we would be able to pay anything off especially, quickly. You will soon see how miraculous 2008 was for us. Remember, we set a few goals to pay some of our debt off by faith only. We knew God would provide the way. In February 2008, Tonya was painting wall murals at the former Tykes, now Stepping Stones Academy; she was finished for the day and was running out the door when she realized she had left her phone on the paint cart. As she was leaving, Punkie, one of her friends and coworkers, was talking with one of the parents when Punkie said, "That's the girl you need to be talking to." She was referring to Tonya.

"What are you getting me into now?" Tonya said to Punkie, laughing of course. Punkie proceeded to tell me this lady's son kept getting sick and had, had RSV, and he just couldn't seem to get well, so she was looking for someone to watch her two sons at her home Mondays through Fridays. I was not looking to add anything else to my already-busy schedule, but she said she would pay me well. I told her I needed to talk it over with my husband and would let her know as soon as possible.

Greg and I talked it over that night, and we felt this was God opening the door to us for part of the income needed to pay off this tremendous debt. I began babysitting and used this money for tithing and paying off debt only. How awesome it is to watch debt melt away. We had decided that the van needed to be paid off first. My family was involved in the car business; knowing how vehicles depreciate and not liking the idea of having a car payment, it would be the best. Our income taxes would help put a huge dent in this debt, the most we had ever received back at the time; we both almost passed out when we found out the amount. This would pay off around $3,500 of the credit card debt and a large chunk of the van. We estimated having the van paid off by May 2008. What a blessing this has been, and the timing was perfect.

Now we could see that we were moving in the direction the Lord wanted us to go, so we started looking for a new place to live. Searching in Raleigh County and coming up short, we both felt the move was going to be bigger. Greg was even checking different states for history teacher openings: South Carolina, Texas, Virginia, and a few others. While he was checking out those, I decided to look for land in Greenbrier County and jokingly informed Greg that there was a piece of land in Dawson with eleven acres in a price range we could afford. Greg just looked at me with this "are you serious?" look and said, "My job is at Independence, and there is no way I would drive it every day."

Since I'm the optimist, I said "No, you can just get a job in Greenbrier County."

Greg just laughed and informed me that there are only four schools he would be qualified to teach at in Greenbrier County, two middle schools and two high schools. History teachers are there for life, so there is not much chance of ever getting a job there, and if there is any opening, most want to hire the local people within the county.

Of course I don't give up that easily, so I tested him and said, "Okay, if there is a history position open, would you be willing to move over that way?"

"I guess," he said along with, "but I just don't foresee it happening." I then pulled up the Greenbrier County Board of Education website job postings, a little shocked I found not only one but two history positions open: one at Eastern Greenbrier Middle School and the other at Greenbrier West High School. I printed them out because I knew Greg would not believe me, especially since I have a long history of pulling jokes on others. I then handed it to him, and we just looked at each other in amazement. "Okay, you need to apply to both, and if this is where the Lord wants us to be, then you will get the job; we will put this totally in God's hands," I said.

Of course he said, "Okay, but I just don't see it happening." The deadline for his application to be in at the board office was just two days away, so we had everything going against us, but it was in God's hands now, and we would let him take care of it all.

Not knowing if he got the job, we decided that we should at least go and look around Greenbrier County for somewhere to live if he were to get the job. Everything we looked at was making us second-guess he was even applying for the position, but it was in God's hands, so we needed to be patient. We received a call approximately a week after he applied; they were asking Greg questions about himself, his degree, and a few other things. Greg looked at this as a formality that all applicants went through, and they let him know they would be making a decision by June 10, 2008, if he got the job; again we would wait. As I was painting at SSA, we received a call that could change our lives. It was the personnel director of Greenbrier County Schools needing to talk to Greg. He was in class, but I knew he needed to talk with him, so I gave him the number to Independence High School and hoped and prayed Greg was able to talk when he called. Waiting again, I knew as soon as Greg spoke with the personnel director he would call me back.

While we wait, I will get you up to speed on other things we were experiencing during all of this. My family had been in the business of setting up Excel modular homes and became friends with the person in charge of ordering them. Mom decided to call him to see if by chance there were any homes that had been built but not claimed. This was a long shot, but we felt it was worth the try. To our surprise, there were four three-bedroom homes and one that could be a five- or six-bedroom home. The three-bedroom homes were sold quickly because there was a greater demand for that size; most do not need all the extra bedrooms. The one that was left would be perfect for us. It was exactly what we were looking for and much more: two and a half bath, large kitchen with a pantry, dining room, family room, office, two-car garage, three-thousand-square-foot home, and all they were asking for it was $95,000. Now this wouldn't include the foundation, septic, well, and some other minor things, but it was an awesome deal for the size home. We were getting a little excited because this house could be put anywhere. Even if Greg didn't get the job in Greenbrier County, we could find a place somewhere. We soon received some discouraging news; the Excel home was sold. What a bummer? We now know we could get this house built within our price range but just not as upgraded as this particular one was. This must have been God's way of letting let us know about it.

Greg finally called to inform me he got the job at Greenbrier West High School, the one he really wanted, but had to turn it down since we could not find anywhere to live. "*What?*" I exclaimed. "Why did you tell them no if you got it? We put this in God's hands, and we're trusting he would take care of us."

"We have been looking for a few weeks, and all we have found are places the same size as ours or dumps. I just think we need to stay where we are, that it may not be what God wants us to do. We can't be homeless; he wouldn't want that," Greg said.

"You have to call them back right now and take the job. After putting this in God's hands and then not taking it after we said if you get the job it is meant for us to move would be like saying to God, 'I don't trust you.' I am scared what God will do if we don't take it," I explained to Greg.

"But they will think I am crazy, and it probably ruined the chance of me getting the job anyway." Greg tried to convince me.

But I said, "I don't care if they think you are crazy. Just explain to them the situation of just being scared that we would be homeless, and they will understand." To make a long story short, Greg called them back and took the job, homeless or not. Who knows, we were now truly walking by faith.

We now needed to step up the process if we were to be in a place and settled by the time school started. A few days after accepting the job, we decided to look at a piece of property that we previously ruled out, only because we thought it was on the main road, Route 60, and we did not want to be close to a main highway. To our surprise, it was in a small subdivision, not located directly on Route 60; the property was three acres, almost completely flat, with a tree and some brush. Perfect, we thought. God's plan is awesome. He had it picked out for us, and it was in our price range, so we made an offer. It was accepted. We needed to now get our home in Midway sold. This could be a chore seeing how the economy had just took a nosedive, and property in the area was sitting; we just had to remember that this was all in God's hands. He would provide. We placed an AD in the local trader and received two calls on our Midway home. One said it was overpriced, and the other said "I want it, I'll pay full price, just please hold it for me while I get financing." So we did. While we were waiting on their approval of financing, we needed to get the Excel home ordered but needed to get the funds for a down payment. The problem with this was no one wanted to finance us until the Midway home was sold, but if we were to be settled in our new lives by the time school started, we needed to get it started. It took six weeks to build it at the plant; then it would have to be finished on site. Our patience was being tested, I believe, because the little things would come up, trying to be stumbling blocks, but we kept trusting God would take care of them, and he did in a way no one could believe. We were just in awe of it all. Tonya's mom got a call that the house we previously knew about was available again. The gentleman who purchased it, a contractor, was unable to take it because the area he wanted it to go in would not allow a permit for a modular home. A piece of paper kept him from buying it. This was in the evening of

June 23, 2008, and mom didn't want to get our hopes up, just in case it didn't work out because it had to be paid for in full by June 30, 2008. I knew we had not finalized the sale of the other house, and the lenders would not bridge the two loans. Mom talked it over with the other family members who were involved with the other Excel homes, and they decided that they would purchase this house for us, then when we sold our Midway house, and we could just pay it back. After mom worked all of this out, she spoke with Greg and I to let us know about this house coming available again. Then mom called a lender they often worked with about the situation, the lender wanted to just try and pull our credit to see if we would be able to do it on our own. To our surprise, she was able to secure the loan on just Greg and I. We had a huge favor to ask her, and we prayed she would be able to pull it off; the loan needed to be closed by Friday June 27, 2008. Keep in mind that this is now Tuesday, June 24, 2008, because the funds had to be in the Excel account by June 30, 2008, closing out their fiscal year with this home off their books. Our lender said, "I'll do what I can. I have never closed a loan in three days, but we will try. I need this...this...and this....to get it started, and I need it by noon. Can you get it here?"

I said, "Sure I will have it there in a few minutes." And off I went.

Are you seeing the work of God here? Be prepared to be amazed because it isn't over yet. As we sat at the closing on Friday June 27, 2008, all who were involved were talking about God's hand in this, just in awe again. We had so much to do: find a contractor to pour the footers, put in the septic and the well, figure out which school the kids will attend, find a church, and who knows what else—all by August 21, 2008. This makes me tired just looking back on all we had to do then. July was a whirlwind, and I do not remember much about it other than preparing for our house to arrive. All the dates are a little fuzzy, but it seems the contractor was not able to start the foundation until mid-July, setting the house began the week of August 4, and the closing of both loans—bridge loan—was August 15, and we were in a time crunch.

The power company was one of our pending problems with getting into our new home, an estimated hookup date of August 28 through September 3. Of course when I called the power company, I gave them my sob story, and the lady said, "Everyone is top priority; you will just have to wait."

We really needed it to be on a week ago because it delayed the contractors a bit having to use generators for their power tools. Ready to accept that the power would not be on until the end of the month, you can understand my excitement when we received a call while at the closing from a gentleman at AEP, informing me that he was just in the area and decided to go ahead and hook up our power line.

"Thank you Jesus!" I shouted, forgetting where I was.

Everyone looked at me a little funny, so of course I proceeded to tell them our story. To God be all the glory, we now have power, six days until Greg had to start work and eight days before the boys would be in school; there was still a lot to do, but God had provided thus far, and we knew he would continue to make the way for us. We were able to finish two of the bedrooms, one to store all of our things in and the other for us all to sleep in, all six of us with five mattresses on the floor; we were in by August 23, so Greg only had to drive it two days, and the boys got to start school on the twenty-sixth.

Our Church Home

And they that are far off shall come and build in the temple of the LORD, and ye shall know that the LORD of hosts hath sent Me unto you. And this shall come to pass if ye will diligently obey the voice of the LORD your God.

Zechariah 6:15

We worked on the house nonstop for the next couple of months: painting, siding, seeding the yard. And with the help of our family members, we finally finished in October. During this time, we wanted to find a church we could call home. We had been invited to five different churches from old friends who live in the area and new friends we just met, but we had been so busy trying to finish up everything we hadn't taken the time to even look. At the beginning of September, Greg was taking Brandon and Ryan to football practice. After dropping them off, he decided to drive around the area; in a little town called Rupert, as he was driving past a little brick church, it almost spoke to him. When he came home, he told me about it, and our conversation went something like this:

"I know where we are going to church this Sunday," Greg said.

"Oh, that is good. Who invited us?" I asked.

"Nobody," he said.

"Well, don't you think we should go to the ones we were invited to first? Where we know someone?" I said to Greg.

"No, this is where I feel God is calling us, so we need to go here. I have trusted your feelings on the move and everything, so trust me on this one. We need to go here," Greg explained.

"Okay, you're right; I'll trust you on this one," I agreed. So we went to this small church called Big Clear Creek Baptist in Rupert, West Virginia.

Sunday we went to this new church, and as we walked into it, we both felt at home—just like we had been there all our lives. We knew we were following God's plan for our lives and felt a peace about it all. That first Sunday we went, they had a guest speaker, an area minister we were familiar with, and it just happened to be their homecoming, so we were invited to eat. We were so thankful for that because we were all tired of eating out. Our stove would not arrive until September 21, and there is only so much you can cook on a griddle—a well-appreciated home-cooked meal along with the company of our new friends in Christ. The message spoke to Greg, and I at that first service, even though it was with the minister we already knew. We decided to go the following Sunday as well to hear the current pastor of that church. Then we would go to a different church the Sunday after because a few of our old friends along with a few new ones attended that particular church, and we had told them we would check it out. Knowing the Lord had already placed us with Big Clear Creek Baptist Church, we went to the other church, not having the same feeling we did as we entered the other church. This was not because it wasn't friendly, because it was quite friendly; it was only because this was not where God wanted us to be. Back at Big Clear Creek Baptist Church the following Sunday, we felt a peace about it all. Still not sure why the big move, this particular church, or other events that took place in the summer of 2008, we were just ready to settle in our new life.

God wants us to take one step at a time trusting him to provide the path. We are so blessed, and it seems like every time we turn around, God is blessing us more. With this new church family, I felt God leading me into youth ministry, although our new church home was lacking in this area, we knew our children would soon benefit from a youth group. I decided to talk to pastor Glen about the concern and decided to give it a try with a handful of children, most middle school–aged and a few high school seniors. God only gives us what we can handle and helps us to grow as we learn. The spring of 2009, I began to do lessons for BYF (Baptist Youth Fellowship); it was not always easy, and the age differences in the group made it more challenging, but with the help of my partner in crime, Linda, they were determined to persevere.

Linda and I have had a lot of fun working with the youth, our group is still small, but we see God working in it. Linda had worked with youth previously and told me about the rallies the local churches participated in. These churches would take turns hosting a rally on the second Monday of each month. Linda thought it would be a good idea to host one at our church; keep in mind I had no clue what I was doing, but God did. The entire group decided we needed to do something unique, and I remembered watching this video on YouTube that was a painting of Jesus to music. I contacted the artist to see if it would be all right to recreate his design for our youth rally, incorporating our youth in part of it and then I would paint it. I had never done this sort of thing before, and faces are not my strong point, but this was to be our program; I had to try. We did a practice run, and it was good for a first try. The next evening would be the real program, it was a hit, and I was blessed through that painting more than you can ever imagine.

Shortly after this painting, I won a CD through our local Christian radio station Spirit FM by the Fee Band. To my surprise, when I listened to this CD, I began to see pictures in my head to paint with the different songs. The first painting I created was given to me by God. (As I am typing this, it came on the satellite radio I am listening to. God is absolutely amazing!) The song on their CD was "Arms That Hold the Universe," and to see if I could paint it, I decided I would let Greg's side of the family be the guinea pigs. At the family reunion in June 2010, I painted "Arms That Hold the Universe"; they all seemed to enjoy it. Many were going through trials I was unaware of at that time but was told later how it blessed them. Since it went over well, I decided to paint it for my dad's family reunion held on Labor Day weekend. It was a hit, and now I could paint it for our next rally, which would be March 14, 2011.

Just before the rally, Linda and I had planned to take the youth group to the junior high convention in Vienna, West Virginia, so off Linda and I went with four boys and one girl on the first weekend in March 2011. We had a wonderful weekend, the girl who went with us was saved, and all of us had fun. The speaker was Brian Burgess, who was amazing and real to the kids. The band Micah Watson Band was awesome and truly a gift from God; of course I purchased both of their CDs with hopes of a new painting inspired by God through their music. We were all excited about the wonderful weekend we had and anxious about getting everything ready for our rally just a week away. To God be the glory! Our rally was wonderful, and God opened a door for me I was not expecting; the painting was quite a blessing. I was asked to come to our Hopewell Association Weekend Camp held in July 2011. They asked if I had any other paintings, and at the time I was working on two from the Micah Watson Band. I told them they were a work in progress, but I should have them ready by that time. I was unaware of the plans that had already been made with the Micah Watson Band planned on being there. When I was informed about this, I became very excited and nervous. They would be playing while I painted. God is amazing!

The more I thought about this, the better I thought the painting could be, especially for the timing of when to paint certain parts. I needed to paint it to see if it would turn out before I contacted the band. Guess what? Family reunion was coming up, they could be my guinea pigs again, and we could record it and see how long it takes.

It Is Well! was the painting I had planned to paint to the old hymn. It was currently on the *Glorious Unveiling* CD by the Micah Watson Band. It came out almost as I envisioned it, and it took sixteen minutes and forty-five seconds the first time I painted it. I soon contacted the band to see if they could extend the song that long, giving me time to paint without it having to be repeated over and over.

To say the least, I was excited for the opportunity to paint with the band and more so after I was around them at camp. At a distance, I wanted to see how they really were, so I watched them, and they truly amazed me. They hung out with the kids, goofing off and playing games with them and really got to know these kids. They are a blessing to others, and God is with them. When I spoke with the different band members, they were all willing to work with me to make the painting what God wanted it to be.

I know how I keep saying how God's timing is best and give it to him. Well, sit back and be amazed once again. I could have never dreamed what was about to happen. I was planning to paint at the end of the evening, but the pastor who was speaking for the weekend changed it up and asked me to open with the painting. Of course, I agreed to do it then and was now even more nervous. As I painted, I felt a peace come over me like it was just me and God. I could hear the music, but I was no longer nervous, and when I finished, I just sat down to listen to the message. Now Greg and I had been praying about where to go with the paintings. I felt God leading me to do them at different events but was not sure if it was what God truly wanted me to do. I asked Greg to be praying about it too. We received an answer that evening when the pastor got up. It was so humbling to me, and God is so powerful. Pastor Allen pointed to the painting and said, crying, "There's my message. When I saw *all my sin* on the cross, I lost it." I know what painting the pictures does for me, but I never dreamed what an impact it could have on others. I was crying, the pastor was crying, and many others were crying. Allen asked for all who needed to lay down anything at the cross to come forward, and to my amazement, close to half the room came forward to pray. God continues to amaze me. Our God will do amazing things for you as well, but you have to give it all to him. Give him the reins; he will lead you where you need to be.

Greg's Thoughts

The move to Greenbrier County was completely driven by the Lord. With the way everything worked out with the land, house, and everything else in the summer of 2008, there was no doubt this was the place we are supposed to be. We then realized that there was a purpose for our move. We knew that we had some work to do for the Lord. He blessed us with a house, job, church; and we felt that we are forever indebted to the Lord. Now I realize we can never out-give or out-bless the Lord; with what he blesses his believers with, there is no way that we could possibly out-give God. However, we knew we had a purpose, mission, and a work to do for the Lord. Tonya started her work at the beginning of 2009 when she and another lady from the church started working with the youth group. All the while I wasn't quite sure what I was supposed to do within the church. I knew there was something I was going to do, not sure of what it was until June 2009. In that month, our regular Sunday school teacher moved on to another church, therefore leaving a vacancy at that position. The next Sunday, we were sitting in our Sunday school class—no teacher, no lesson, just talking. Then Linda, she's the person who leads the youth group along with Tonya, said, "We need to figure out what to do about our Sunday school class and a teacher." I knew the answer; I realized immediately this was what I was supposed to do for God. I remember sitting there with my head down when Linda spoke, and it felt like everyone in the room was looking at me and expecting me to answer. Whether people were looking at me or not, I do not know, but I do know that the eyes of the Lord were burning through me. I had to speak up and accept the position. I didn't know what to expect, but I was trusting in the Lord to direct my teaching of the class. He hasn't failed me in that task. He has blessed me so much that I look forward to Sunday mornings and teaching Sunday school; I love it. Even though I was reluctant to take the class—after all, we were still new to the church—all it took was for me to step out in faith, and God did the rest. At the time of this writing, I am still teaching the class, I have become a trustee of the church, and I assist Tonya with her paintings in whatever capacity she needs my help. Our leap of faith has reaped magnificent rewards for us and me personally. I have no regrets.

Our Future

Although we do not know what the future holds, we plan to continue on the path the Lord leads us on. Only the Lord knows where it leads. Please be in prayer for us and our family so that we stay faithful to the Lord in all we do. Make every day count and do everything for the Lord now.

May the Lord bless you and your family as He has for us!

Extra Blessings

We had to add this little extra blessings part to share some of the other blessings in our lives; be prepared to be amazed once again.

A Miracle for Ryan

When Ryan weighted 8 pounds and 2.4 ounces when he was born. He was a nice-size baby boy. Shortly after he was born, he quit growing, and his doctor was unsure why. He had numerous tests ran all coming up negative. We knew he had hernias just as both of his older brothers had, but they did not want him having surgery until he started growing or until they figured out what was wrong with him. The reason for not doing the surgery was based on concern that he would not come out of the anesthesia. He was a high risk for SIDS (sudden infant death syndrome); this scared me to death. I did not sleep for months worrying about this, and I am not usually a worrier. To make a long story short, I went over what his pediatrician said and scheduled an appointment with the surgeon that his brothers saw anyway. The day before his appointment, I could not get him to quit crying. Anyone with children knows when their child is in pain, and this was a hurting cry. I tried everything to calm him, but he would not quit, and I got a knock on my door. It was one of my sisters-in-law, her mom had gotten a prayer cloth from revival, it was prayed over for Ryan that night or the night before. She said, "I thought Ryan might need it." She had no clue he had been crying all day.

I immediately took it and laid it under his little head and prayed, "Lord, I give Ryan to you, to do as you see fit. We do not know what is wrong with him, but I know you do, so he is yours , Lord." I did not know if my baby was going to make it or not; he was not gaining weight. At four months, he was only ten pounds and gained less than two in four months. He threw up more than he took in and was so tiny. It is still hard for me to look back without getting teary eyed. I decided to change his diaper again, and when I did, I was in shock; his sack had turned coal black. I immediately called my cousin who worked for the surgeon to see if I should wait for his appointment since it was one of the first appointments the next morning or go on to the hospital. In a calm voice, she said, "I think you should go ahead and take him to the ER, and I will call the doctor just to let him know you are on your way so he can meet you there."

I got him ready, and his dad and I went to the hospital. I found out later that as soon as my cousin hung up with me, she called the doctor. She was scared for Ryan, because with it turning black it meant something went in where the hernia was and could have caused major damage if not treated immediately. She didn't tell me as I lived forty-five minutes from the hospital and had to go over a decent-size mountain; she wanted me to get to the hospital safely. When we arrived at the hospital, it was nearly midnight; Ryan was prepped and in surgery in less than fifteen minutes, then back in my arms about an hour later. All of his problems were stemmed from the hernias, and after his surgery, he was able to hold down his food and started growing again. They told us that he was in so much pain from the hernias he could not hold down the food because he was staying nauseated. This happened in December 1999.

In January, his pediatrician wanted to see him for a checkup. During this checkup, she was listening to his heartbeat longer than usual. She heard a heart murmur, so she ordered more tests: EKG and a few others I can't remember. He had these tests on January 6, 2000, and it was confirmed he had two small holes in his heart. I was devastated, but I gave it all over to the Lord, and at church that next Sunday, I had him prayed over and anointed with oil. The doctor scheduled an appointment with a child cardiologist who came to Beckley the last week of every month; a day before his appointment that doctor wanted another set of tests ran to compare them with the ones from January 6. After carefully looking over both sets of tests on Ryan, he confirmed that a miracle had taken place. Both holes had closed, and he gave him a clean bill of health. The doctor actually said it was a miracle from God. The first tests clearly showed two holes, and he informed me the size of the holes could not have closed that fast without help from God. He said the smaller one would normally take about six to eight months to close all the way, and if the other would not have closed by age two, he would have had to have surgery. God is amazing! He still performs miracles today; Ryan is a miracle from God and a blessing.

Gas or Groceries

We have had a lot of amazing things happen in life, and this one Greg remembered. He said we needed to add it, and after he refreshed my memory, I agreed. We were almost out of money, but we needed some groceries. We realized on our way to get the groceries that the van was on E—actually below E—but we went to the store anyway, praying we did not run out of gas with the kids in the car. We got to the store, got the bare necessities, and wondered how in this world we would get home without running out of gas. We got back out to the van, and—lo and behold— we had nearly half a tank of gas. Our God never ceases to amaze us; we were able to drive on that gas until Greg got his paycheck a day or so later. Don't underestimate God!

The Check in the Mail

Greg's car needed work, and we did not have the money to pay for it when it was finished. We were not expecting it to be as much as it was, so we left the car at the shop until school was getting ready to start. We did not want to ask our family for any more help, although they would have. A few days before school started, we received a check for a little more than the bill, so we were able to get his car back and not rely on anyone but God. He will provide if we allow him, putting it all in his hands.

By the way, the check was from an overpaid bill, not a mysterious sender check. I never overpaid bills. We didn't have it, so we could not; I know God worked that one out.

Looking back at all the different dates, we purposely wrote exact dates, so you could see how God's plan was in motion even when we were young children and teens.

For more information about Greg and Tonya and their ministry, visit: www.TheInspirationalExpressions.com.